How to Stop Being Defensive

Step-by-Step Guide on How to Take Criticism Positively, Stop Being Toxic, Stop Being Passive Aggressive, and Stop Being Selfish To Keep Your Relationships Healthy and Alive

Introduction

No one can say life is an easy ride. We all know that it's full of ups and downs, many of which teach us great lessons. Unfortunately, we often adopt an unhealthy attitude towards our problems and mistakes, and unknowingly, we start developing a defense system in the brain.

This defense mechanism is our way of handling judgments and censure. It causes us to react to criticism, act irrationally, lash out at others, act selfishly at times, and keeps us from benefitting from positive advice.

We start to develop a behavioral trait called 'defensive behavior.' At times, this trait can be protective. However, on most occasions, it negatively impacts your behavior and weakens your relationships.

If this resonates with you, and being defensive has negatively impacted your personal and professional life, there's hope! You can turn things around!

This book is a complete guide on how to control defensive behavioral traits. In it, you'll find actionable information and potent strategies you can use to:

- *Overcome defensive behavior*

- *Stop being selfish and toxic with others*
- *Take criticism constructively*
- *Improve passive-aggressive behavior and anger management issues, and*
- *Become a more positive individual who receives criticism openly to work towards betterment.*
- ***And so much, much more!***

Beginning this journey will help you become a wiser and more confident person. Let's get started:

Table of Content

Introduction _____ 2

Chapter 1: Understanding Defensive Behavior and its Consequences _____ 7

    What is Defensive Behavior? _____ 7

    Why Defensive Behavior Develops _____ 9

    How Defensive Behavior Impacts Relationships 10

Chapter 2: How To Stop Being Passive Aggressive _____ 15

    What is Passive Aggressive Behavior? _____ 15

    How to Control and Overcome Passive Aggressiveness _____ 17

Chapter 3: Learn Better Anger Management to Stop Being Defensive _____ 22

    The Negative Effects of Anger Management __ 22

    The Most Effective Anger Management Strategies _____ 25

How to Become Emotionally Masterful _____ 29

Chapter 4: How to Handle Criticism Positively _____ 31

Constructive Criticism _____ 32

Destructive Criticism _____ 32

The Benefits of Handling Criticism Well _____ 33

How to Handle Positive Criticism Positively ___ 36

Chapter 5: How to Stop Being Toxic and Selfish _____ 42

Common Traits of Toxic People _____ 42

How to Stop Being Toxic and Selfish _____ 45

Chapter 7: How to Identify and Overcome Your Weaknesses and Shortcomings _____ 54

How to Identify Your Weaknesses and Shortcomings _____ 55

How to Overcome Your Weakness and Shortcomings _____ 59

Chapter 8: Growth Mindset: Why and How you Must Develop it _____ 68

What Is A Growth Mindset? _____ 69

Importance of Growth Mindset _____ 69

How the Fixed Mindset Limits You _____ 71

How to Develop a Growth Mindset _____ 75

Chapter 9: Positive Habits to Improve Defensive Behavior _____ 80

Conclusion _____ 84

Chapter 1: Understanding Defensive Behavior and its Consequences

In life, you come across situations where you have to stand alone and be your own hero to protect yourself. To do so, you develop specific behavioral traits that always help you win.

Whether you do it by being polite or showing anger, you develop a self-mechanism called defensive behavior to protect your physical and mental state.

This chapter will help you understand what defensive behavior is, how you develop it, and its effects on your life.

What is Defensive Behavior?

Let's break the term defensive behavior into two parts: ***defensive*** and ***behavior***.

Defensive means to guard, protect, or shield; on the other hand, behavior refers to how you act. Thus, we can say that defensive behavior means to act in a certain meant to protect you.

Your personality, beliefs, personal experiences, and attitude contribute to building defensive behavior. For example, as a child, whenever someone told you 'no,' you started shouting or crying, pressurizing the other person to fulfill your demand. By doing so, you learned a method of getting your way.

Defensive behavior is how you respond to a threat. For example, when you perceive people with more potential than you as a threat—it can be your colleague, classmate, sibling, spouse, or someone appreciated by other people— you act defensively.

If anyone tries to prove you wrong during a discussion, you switch on your defensive behavior and keep proving your point until the next person gives up. Your ego doesn't allow the other person to win.

This behavior closely relates to how other people treat you and the kind of life you've lived. You find an escape from the negativities of life by fighting them with rage.

Since you now understand what defensive behavior is, let's discuss why you develop it.

Why Defensive Behavior Develops

There are numerous reasons why defensive behavior develops. Here're various of them:

- Insecurities in life and the fear of losing what you have makes you defensive. Consider an instance where your friend starts socializing with other peers, which develops feelings of insecurity that he/she might leave you. Out of the fear of 'being friendless,' you become controlling and force your friend to choose between you and the new friends.

- You may also adopt this defensive behavior to protect yourself emotionally and physically as the only person you care about is yourself. For example, when your spouse wants to wear a dress of her choice, not yours, her 'no' may trigger your defensive behavior, and you start debating on why she should prefer wearing the dress you suggested.

- You may act defensively as a means to avoid heartbreak. When you're afraid of getting hurt, you become defensive whenever things don't go your way and avoid facing the situation.

- The feeling of superiority forces you to act defensively. If you always like having the upper hand and receiving acknowledgment and appreciation for everything you do, you'll feel tempted to keep proving your point until the next person surrenders.

- You are always ready to defend your ego as hearing 'no' as an answer has never been an option.

To satisfy your ego, you build a defense mechanism to such an extent that it starts affecting your relationships. Nobody enjoys feeling pressured and controlled. When you're too controlling, you drive other people away.

Now let's discuss how defensive behavior weakens your relationships:

How Defensive Behavior Impacts Relationships

The satisfaction of always hearing a 'yes' increases the intensity of your defensive behavior. You start finding ways to intimidate others so that they fear saying 'no' to you. Unfortunately, when things get to that point, it becomes impossible to see your behavior's adverse effects on your relations because the power of superiority has blinded you.

Your defensive behavior helps shield your ego, yes, but it often takes a toll on your well-being and life in the following ways.

It makes other people feel worthless

When you're defensive, you always eager to tell others how intelligent and smart you are. You always praise yourself and are never willing to accept your mistake. This habit makes others feel worthless, which can have adverse effects on your relationships—to the point of ruining intimacy.

For example, you and your colleague worked on a project that turned out to be a great success. Instead of appreciating the colleague's efforts, you take all the credit instead because you can't tolerate having other people appreciated in your presence.

It keeps you from taking criticism positively

As a defensive person, you're likely to find criticism insulting. Instead of taking criticism positively and using it as fodder for self-improvement, you end up fighting with the other person.

Imagine yourself in a meeting where your boss gives you advice on what you can do to improve your presentation skills. Instead of taking his criticism positively, you start arguing to prove him wrong. In the process, you risk your job and destroy your image.

Similarly, the tendency to overreact to criticism and perceive it negatively affects other areas of your life.

You may get into heated arguments with loved ones because they try to give you suggestions on how to be better, or even when they are casually giving you advice. For example, when your spouse tells you that you look great in black instead of blue, you react to the suggestions defensively, perhaps by telling your spouse that you look good in everything.

You blame others

When you develop defensive behavioral tendencies, you tend to blame others for your mistakes and avoid taking responsibility for your decisions and actions.

Since you believe you are good at everything and can never be wrong, you find it easy to blame others for your problems. For example, when you forget to buy tickets for the movie you'd promised to buy while your friend buys movie snacks, instead of apologizing, you blame him/her for not reminding you about the tickets.

You avoid confronting situations

Whenever you know you are wrong but cannot handle the truth of the matter/situation, you always leave. You tend to avoid confronting situations, leaving your loved ones in distress.

You avoid facing the truth to protect your ego by running away from the situation because it seems like the easier way out. Although you feel fine running away from confronting situations, you deeply loath this behavior, and it upsets you.

You're judgmental

Being defensive makes you judgmental of people and all situations. You judge others for things they haven't done just to make them feel insecure and yourself superior. Constantly judging other people makes them feel unimportant and worthless, pushing them away from you.

For example, after your coworker creates an excellent presentation and receives praise for his efforts, you take his presentation as a threat to your job and start demeaning him to make yourself feel better.

The traits mentioned above harm both your personality and your relationships. If you examine your life in light of these situations, they will resonate with you. You will realize how your defensive behavior is interfering with your well-being and growth, which does not sit well with you.

If you want to live a better life, you have to improve your passive-aggressiveness, which is one of the main aspects of defensive behavior.

In the next chapter, we'll discuss ways to control your emotions and how to stop being passive-aggressive.

Chapter 2: How To Stop Being Passive Aggressive

Defensiveness creates an emotional state conducive to developing many other adversarial behavioral traits, one of which is passive-aggressiveness. Passive aggressiveness is an unhealthy behavior that has a negative influence on your behavior and life.

Let us explore it further in this chapter and discuss strategic approaches you can use to control and correct the behavior:

What is Passive Aggressive Behavior?

Passive aggression is a behavioral trait where you show your aggression indirectly. Instead of directly expressing or discussing what's bothering you, you show your resentment through anger, ignorance, or in any other way, confusing the other person.

Researchers believe that passive aggression starts developing in childhood. As children, guardians and parents often teach us not to express anger or any emotion considered "wrong."

Thus, instead of learning how to express emotions, we start hiding them. Parenting style, harsh punishments, neglect, or child abuse might cause the development of passive aggression.

Take an example where your friends plan a trip, but you are not interested. Instead of voicing your opinion, you agree with the plan and go along with them. However, since you were against the plan, you resist enjoying it. You might make excuses in joining them or tell them how badly they planned the trip, showing your disagreement.

Passive aggression is a behavioral disorder that affects your ability to maintain healthy personal and work relationships. Below are a few common signs of passive-aggressive behavior:

- You have a pessimistic approach to life.
- You frequently complain about not feeling appreciated enough.
- You often act stubbornly.
- When someone questions your opinion, you act rude and irritable.
- You keep blaming others for your mistakes.

Passive-aggressive behavior pushes your friends and family away. Because you start sending out negative vibes, other people start steering clear off and ignoring you. You don't show respect towards other peoples' emotions and are likely to throw tantrums at the slightest of provocations.

Now that you understand passive-aggressive behavior, let's discuss ways to overcome it.

How to Control and Overcome Passive Aggressiveness

If you want to overcome passive-aggressive behavior for good, you need to start expressing your feelings in positive ways.

Here are some approaches you can use to cope with, control, and overcome passive aggression:

#: *Observe your Behavior*

The best way to overcome passive aggression is by observing your behavior and become more aware of the situations that trigger your aggressive behavior.

For example, imagine you're attending a conference, and it's your turn to give your input. The fear of disappointing others compels you to act passive-aggressively. Instead of sharing your views, you try changing the topic or, worse, leave the conference.

Start observing the different environmental factors and situations, including people, ideas, and events that trigger your passive behavior so that you can learn to tackle them better.

#: *Be expressive*

Firstly, you need to start expressing how you feel and openly share your emotions. Nobody can guess what you are going through until you share. Once you start becoming expressive, people can understand you better and treat you the way you want.

For example, when you are angry with your friend Jim who is unaware that he has hurt you, instead of hiding your emotions, you can tell him why you are angry, giving him a chance to defend himself.

By being emotionally expressive, you learn to act sanely and secure your relations. Here are a few tips you can use to express yourself in a better way:

- **Try responding instead of reacting to your emotions:** When you feel triggered, understand how you feel, give yourself time, and try finding ways to handle the situation better. For example, if you feel upset about moving away from your friends and family, instead of crying and throwing tantrums, spend quality time with your loved ones and tell them how you feel.

- **Express yourself creatively either by painting, dancing, or writing:** By indulging in healthy, creative activities, you explore yourself, finding better ways to express yourself. When in distress, play some happy music and dance. Smile and move your muscles in every direction. Doing this calms you by releasing tension from your body.

- **Talk to yourself; after all, nobody understands you better than you do:** When you feel distressed, self-discuss the problem and ways to settle the situation without creating a scene.

#: *Be assertive*

Learn to be assertive instead of pessimistic. Assertive behavior gives you the confidence to express how you feel boldly without putting your sanity at risk.

For example, when your partner asks you to join him in watching his favorite movie, which you have no interest in, you should openly share your disagreement of the pick, not pick a fight or start an argument. By doing so, you'll avoid hurt feelings all around and can even settle on a movie that meets both your preferences.

To be assertive, first, get clarity of how you feel and what you want to do. Once you understand that, you can then act accordingly.

Take an instance where you and your partner are thinking about moving to another city, but the idea isn't sitting well with you because you will have to leave your job and friends. In that case, you should analyze the situation, understand what you want, and then assertively discuss your point with your partner.

#: *Give yourself space*

Giving yourself space is as important as giving it to others. By doing so, you accept your flaws and give yourself time to improve. It's not wise to be physically present in a situation that triggers your passive-aggressive tendencies. If you feel triggered, excuse yourself and take time to understand how you feel. Once you're in control of your emotions, you can clear the matter.

For example, if you are angry at your colleague for not preparing the presentation on time, it is best to take some time off from him/her instead of being around him/her, getting triggered in the process.

Try using these methods and observe the positive changes they help you make. The main cause of both passive and defensive behavior is your uncontrolled anger, which means 'anger management' is one of the best ways to stop being defensive and passive-aggressive.

Let's discuss how anger management helps you handle your emotions:

Chapter 3: Learn Better Anger Management to Stop Being Defensive

Anger has received a bad rap for many years, but the reality is that it's just an emotion. In actuality, your reaction is what turns anger into a negative or positive emotion. If you get into a fight with a friend because you feel angry at him/her for being rude to you, your reaction channelizes the anger into negative energy.

It is vital to learn how to control your anger and harness it positively instead of venting it out irrationally or suppressing it to a point where it turns into something monstrous.

Let us understand better how being short-tempered ruins your life and why you need to exercise better anger management to leash in defensiveness and passive-aggressiveness.

The Negative Effects of Anger Management

Your lack of control over your emotions makes you short-tempered, which is an inclination to showing anger over small issues.

When you're short-tempered, you react angrily to almost everything and never stop to analyze whether something is worth the anger or not. Everything and everyone starts threatening your mental peace, forcing you to react.

Here are some side effects of reacting or suppressing anger:

- High-stress levels, something common with anger, make you susceptible to heart disease, diabetes, high blood pressure, and a weakened immune system.

- Chronic anger consumes your energy, resulting in poor concentration, fatigue, depression, and chronic anxiety.

- Your anger scars your relationships because uncontrolled anger causes hurtful words and actions, making it hard for others to trust you.

Becoming mindful of the signs/triggers that cause anger-driven outbursts or reactions is one of the first things you need to do to start managing anger.

A few small physical changes take place in your body when you feel angry. They include:

- The feeling of having knots in the stomach

- Your face turns red

- You clench your fists and jaws

- Getting headaches or migraines
- Heavy breathing
- Your muscles tighten up
- Your heartbeat increases
- You can't concentrate

Observe your behavior for these signs so that you can gain a better understanding of how you feel.

If you have a hot temper and think you can never handle the emotion, you are wrong. You have more control over your anger than you think; all you need to know is the right, calming strategies to use.

Let's discuss strategies you can use for anger management:

The Most Effective Anger Management Strategies

To become better at anger management:

#: *Start a countdown*

A countdown is one of the easiest and most effective ways to manage anger. Here's the gist of it: **when you feel angry, start counting to ten, and if you feel super furious, count to a hundred.**

For example, if a waiter spills soda on your dress, infuriating you, instead of reacting, glue your lips together and start counting, and keep counting until your anger subsides.

The countdown method diverts your attention from the actual issue towards numbers, and by the time you stop counting, you've forgotten why you were feeling angry in the first place.

#: *Breath deeply*

When you're angry, your breathing intensifies, and you start breathing fast and rapidly as your anger increases. During moments of anger, try reversing your breathing pattern.

Instead of breathing fast, breathe slowly. Inhale deeply, filling your lungs, and then slowly exhale from your mouth.

Engaging in this exercise shifts your attention to your breathing pattern, giving you time to compose your mind.

#: Get involved in an activity

When you feel angry, immediately involve yourself in another activity. Find a good distraction like calling a friend, going for a walk, listening to music, or any other activity that keeps you calm.

For instance, if James made you angry, don't react; try calling a friend instead. Tell your trusted friend about how you feel, and try to make the conversation healthy—perhaps about what you can do to resolve the interpersonal conflict.

#: Relax your muscles

Anger causes your muscles to become stiff and tight, especially your neck and shoulder muscles.

When you become aware of this, try relaxing them by bending your neck on both sides and moving your shoulders in a circular motion; relaxing your muscles signals your mind to calm down too.

#: Repeat a mantra

An anger easing mantra can be a lifesaver.

When you feel angry, close your eyes and start repeating your mantra, which can be any word or phrase that cools you down. For instance, your mantra could be, "I am calm—or simply 'calm.'" Whenever you feel triggered, start chanting your mantra, 'I am calm,' and let it do the magic.

#: *Embrace solitude*

Sometimes the best way to handle anger is to seek some alone time. When you feel that a situation is getting out of hand, stirring your defensiveness and aggression, remove yourself from the situation.

Sit alone, breathe, and take your time to understand how you feel and how to respond to what you're feeling. Solitude makes you focus on your emotions, helping you make the best decision.

#: *Journal your feelings*

You cannot share or control your emotions every time you feel anger. Sometimes it's easy to write down the things you can't, don't want to say, or when said, can have adverse effects.

By writing down your feelings, you transfer your emotions from your mind into a piece of paper. You can keep a journal with you at all times and jot down your emotions, such as anger, as you experience them.

#: Prioritize your relationships

Your priorities significantly influence your decisions and actions. If you prioritize yourself, you won't feel motivated to control anger because you'll always want to win, distancing your loved ones in the process. If you want to sustain your relationships, you have to prioritize them.

When you prioritize your relationships, you try your best to make them work by respecting and understanding your loved ones. For example, when your relationship is a priority, and you know that certain behaviors upset your spouse, you won't try to fight and justify yourself. Instead, you will admit your mistake , apologize, and commit to being a better person.

These strategies were all about helping you learn how to manage anger in the best way possible.

Another factor that triggers anger is a lack of emotional self-control. When you don't know how to handle or manage your emotions, it's easy to give them a chance to get the better of you, thereby worsening an already bad situation.

We live in a world that doesn't give importance to emotional education, where some emotions have become specific to men and women, making expressing emotions that much more challenging.

We grow up hearing statements such as 'men don't cry' or 'don't be angry,' or 'that's bad.' Such doctrines make you conscious and embarrassed about expressing how you feel.

That doesn't have to be the case:

Below are a few ways that will help you handle your emotions in healthy ways.

How to Become Emotionally Masterful

To become a better emotional manager:

#: *Identify your emotion*

You experience thousands of emotions in a day but can only identify very few of them, which is one of the main causes of emotional distress. You must start identifying emotions such as anger, happiness, and excitement; that's the only way to understand them better.

For example, if you feel uncomfortable in Lily's presence, before showing any reaction, tell yourself how you feel. If you feel anger and resentment, before you start yelling at her, talk to her and sort things out. This way, you will learn to understand your emotions and handle the situation maturely.

#: *Let it out*

You should start embracing your emotions by expressing them. Never fear expressing how you feel. Start sharing your emotions with someone you trust. For example, whenever you feel upset, share it with a friend or cry your heart out. By doing so, you let go of your emotions and feel normal again.

Try following these methods and observe the change in your behavior. As you improve on that, you'll start being calmer, which will improve your ability to take criticism constructively.

Let's delve into that a bit more deeply in the next chapter:

Chapter 4: How to Handle Criticism Positively

Let's face it; as we all have, you've faced criticism at this or the other stage of your life. From childhood to adulthood, you often hear all the 'dos' and 'don'ts' of living in a society.

In this process, you often tend to develop an unaccepting attitude towards criticism because it causes self-doubt and causes you to question your motives as negative thoughts start to mount your mind. Your defensive attitude makes you ignore criticism as it lowers your self-esteem and creates self-doubt.

That said, if you continue adopting a negative attitude towards criticism, you may miss many helpful pieces of advice and information that can help you be better in life. Not every critique is bad, and often, people offer you their analysis and suggestions to help you grow.

As you make your way towards self-improvement and success, it is crucial to learn how to differentiate between constructive and unconstructive criticism and take both positively.

Before we discuss how to handle criticism, let's learn about the two types of criticism: constructive and destructive criticism.

Constructive Criticism

Positive criticism, also called 'constructive criticism,' is feedback based on facts and provides improvement suggestions. It consists of tips, advice, strategies, or specific recommendations to initiate positive outcomes, creating a positive atmosphere.

More importantly, this kind of criticism has a supportive and amicable tone and environment. People who genuinely wish to see you grow offer healthy critique in an assuring manner, ensuring you don't feel bad about it and can use the advice well.

For instance, in the workplace, constructive criticism can be your boss providing improvement strategies to help you and your colleagues achieve their targets.

Destructive Criticism

Destructive criticism is the opposite of constructive criticism and is mostly full of rage and envious feelings. While destructive criticism may have some actual words of wisdom, the ulterior motive behind destructive criticism is to demoralize you and shatter your confidence. You are likely to get destructive criticism from a competitive coworker, self-centered spouse, or an envious friend.

For instance, if your coworker consistently demeans you so that he can get that promotion by shifting your attention toward his negative comments, that's him throwing destructive criticism your way. Try avoiding the company of such people and ignore their criticism.

While you should ignore destructive criticism, it is important to tackle positive criticism with an accepting attitude.

The Benefits of Handling Criticism Well

Here are a few benefits of handling criticism positively.

A chance to improve yourself

People criticize you as they evaluate you on specific standards, whether of their own or that of an organization, i.e., your job. Please always take criticism as an opportunity and work on your weakness.

If your boss tells you to emend or improve your presentation, that doesn't mean your efforts are not appreciated. Take it as an opportunity to make it more interesting and impactful.

Understand others care for you

People who truly care for you and want to see you flourish help you improve by pointing out your shortcomings because they know your true potential. You need to understand that not everyone criticizes to insult you.

Often, loved ones criticize to bring out the best in you. Take an example where you decide to wear a green dress for a funeral, and your friend disagrees with your choice. Instead of fighting or getting defensive, think about the embarrassment your friend saved you from by ensuring that you don't wear that dress to a funeral.

Instead of reacting irrationally, try considering criticism as a positive form of love.

It helps you analyze yourself

Criticism helps you analyze yourself and find your mistakes before anyone else does. It helps you become your "own judge" by keenly observing yourself in every field.

For instance, before submitting your project, you can self-examine it at least twice or thrice. You carefully choose your dress according to the occasion. You think multiple times before expressing your thoughts to avoid being the laughing stock.

Improves relationships

Criticism is very beneficial, especially at work and improving your relationships, because it helps you identify your weak points.

In actuality, people who criticize you care for you and want to see you succeed in life. They stop you from making mistakes because they know your limitless potential. If your colleague or manager criticizes your performance, his/her main motive may be to keep you motivated.

People admire you

When you start learning from criticism, you become emotionally and mentally strong, creating a strong and positive character or image. People become more comfortable in sharing their thoughts without any argument.

When you don't react to the input, feedback, and suggestions other people offer, you come off as an amicable and understanding individual who people admire and respect.

Now let's discuss how you can handle criticism positively.

How to Handle Positive Criticism Positively

Being incompetent at handling criticism keeps you from tapping into growth opportunities. Additionally, when you constantly overreact to positive words of advice from loved ones, that strains your bond with them.

Fortunately, you can improve your life and mental health by learning how to handle criticism positively.

Here are some good ways to get started with that:

#: Don't lash back

If your first reaction to criticism is to fight back and be defensive, take a minute before you react. It's normal to feel bad after receiving criticism, but what's more important is to understand if the criticism is positive or negative. If it's negative, ignore it and if it's constructive, learn from it. Lashing back makes you appear intolerant towards others.

For instance, if your partner suggests ways to improve your cooking skills, take it positively, understanding that your partner will always want the best for you.

#: Find positivity in negativity

You must learn to focus on the positive aspects of life. Ignoring destructive criticism is hard as it erodes your self-esteem and respect, but it is the right thing to do. By focusing on negativity, you allow others to win and intimidate you. Always take negative criticism as positive by proving other peoples' judgment wrong.

Spend time with positive people, acknowledging their positive criticism. If someone suggests something to you, think of how it could help you improve, and if someone is only trying to put you down, ignore the demeaning behavior, but analyze the advice given, and if it has a positive lesson, adopt it.

If your peer constantly drags you into every conversation, saying hurtful things, don't react to him/her. Prove the person wrong by obtaining high grades or by getting that promotion.

#: *Learn from criticism*

You must understand that you are not perfect because nobody is or can ever be perfect. There is always room for improvement, both personally and professionally. When you receive criticism, take time to process the criticism, not the person, and focus on what you can learn from it.

If you believe you need no improvement, you are wrong. We all have weaknesses and shortcomings we can improve. Your drive to learn, but the more you drive, the more you learn.

Criticism is the same: the more you focus on what it can teach you, the better you'll be.

Whenever someone offers you any censure and critique, think about how it highlights your weaknesses, and look for ways to improve them. For example, if a client gives you his feedback on an order that you didn't deliver on time, don't try to justify the late delivery. Instead, understand how that may be a business shortcoming and take steps to overcome it, such as providing a better customer experience, thus widening your customer base.

#: Don't take criticism too personally

We tend to feel personally offended when we receive criticism. We perceive it as a personal insult or challenge meant to attack our self-esteem.

You must understand this:

Not every criticism comes from the desire to demotivate you; most criticism comes from wanting to see you improve. If someone tells you to work hard, be punctual, or become friendlier, no matter how that criticism comes across, it is positive and meant to help you succeed in every field of life.

Moreover, sometimes people may vent out their frustration by criticizing you. A colleague who is also a friend may be upset about being late to work due to being stuck in traffic and may take out his/her annoyance on you by reminding you of your project's problems.

In such times, understand that the other person is going through a hard time and ignore his/her negativity. If he/she intentionally or unintentionally points out your areas of improvement, accept them openly, and work on them.

#: Listen with an open mind

Actively listen to the feedback given to you, keeping your ego aside. Understand that people often gave good intentions and hear them out. If you feel triggered, take a deep calming breath.

People usually criticize you because they want to help you improve or learn. Remember, the primary purpose of criticism from your friends and family is to see you make progress in life. Whenever and no matter how they voice this advice, stay calm to avoid reacting. You never know from where life-changing advice shall come; none of us does.

#: Be thankful for getting valuable critique

No matter how bad the criticism makes you feel, always thank the other person and respond with a smile, surprising them with your optimistic approach. Practice patience and mindfulness to help you deal with criticism positively.

For example, if your coworker critically analyzes your work maliciously intending to erode your self-respect, respond with a smile, and ignore it instead of showing bitterness; that's the greatest victory.

#: *Smile*

A smile is the best weapon against pessimism. The best way to respond to criticism is by smiling, thereby communicating to other people how little their words impact your life.

Smiling diverts your attention from criticism to positivity and makes your atmosphere positive, helping you develop a positive life approach. The next time someone criticizes you, smile as widely as you can, say thank you for the valuable input, and move on.

The best thing you can do for yourself is to gradually develop the ability to take criticism as a part of life and take it as a chance to identify your mistakes and become a better person. The more you work on this area, the faster you'll find yourself growing better in different aspects of life and achieving great success.

As you become more receptive towards and handle criticism constructively, you'll notice a massive improvement in your defensive behavior. To keep that momentum growing, work on overcoming your tendency to become selfish and act toxic with others.

The following chapter delves deeper into this aspect of your behavior:

Chapter 5: How to Stop Being Toxic and Selfish

Over time, defensive behavior covertly distills hate, recklessness, and anxiousness into your behavior, making you a selfish person in certain ways. You build walls around yourself, isolating yourself from loved ones. By doing so, you surround yourself with negativity, filling your mind with toxicity. You only do as you please, prioritizing yourself always.

In the process of being toxic and selfish, you lose your hold on life and your emotions. Your stubbornness stops you from seeking help or admitting your mistakes. When your toxicity suffocates you, only then do you realize the mess you have created.

Before finding a solution to your problem, you must learn some common traits of toxic people and identify if you have any.

Common Traits of Toxic People

Being toxic makes you want to dominate other people, often pushing them to their limits. Below are traits common in toxic people:

Are manipulative

You never develop relationships or engage in any activity without having a motive. Whatever you do is well planned and meant to help you accomplish ulterior motives. In such cases, you use people to fulfill your needs. You manipulate others and don't believe in treating them as equals.

For example, you prove yourself innocent by blaming your partner for your relationship problems. You make him/her feel guilty and not leave you while you keep feeding your ego.

Resort to emotional blackmail

A toxic personality makes you an emotional manipulator. To meet your needs, you use guilt trips and emotionally blackmail other people. Consider a divorced parent who stops you from spending time with your other parent so that they don't lose your custody. They play with your emotions by telling you how lonely they are or how your other parent has hurt them over the years. Or think of your significant other who threatens to harm themselves physically if you leave.

Blame others and avoid responsibility

You never take responsibility for your actions and emotional reactions. Instead of finding a solution, you blame other people. You come up with elaborated explanations, justifying yourself as innocent. Your endless blame game forces other people to apologize for something they haven't done.

For example, you may keep blaming your partner for their dominating behavior, give justifications when proven wrong, and skirting the need to apologize for your mistakes.

You never apologize because you believe you're never in the wrong. You never acknowledge your mistakes, believing everything is someone else's fault.

Constant criticism

You constantly criticize others as a coping mechanism to your insecurities—to feel less insecure. Your insecurities and inability to live a successful life makes you envious of others. You pull others down by dragging them in your meaningless conversations, shattering their confidence.

These are a few traits common in toxic people. Do you notice any of them in your personality?

If you do, how has that affected your life? Are you tired of living alone? Are you willing to end your toxic behavior? If so, then keep reading as we discuss ways to stop being toxic and selfish:

How to Stop Being Toxic and Selfish

Toxic behavior can be a constant threat to other people who want to live a peaceful life. You must have the will to develop the courage to stop being toxic and selfish as this journey won't be easy. To prevent your relations from becoming toxic, you need to develop new habits, keeping your connection strong.

Let's discuss approaches you can use to replace a toxic personality with a more pleasing one:

#: Don't be passive-aggressive

As discussed earlier, Passive aggression means showing your disagreement indirectly. Because we've already discussed passive aggression in previous chapters, let's discuss a few examples of how it makes you toxic.

Consider an instance where a friend asks you to join her for a horror movie marathon. Even though you hate horror movies but don't want to hurt your friend's feelings, you unwillingly agree to join in on the 'fun.' As you watch the movies, you constantly complain about how bad the plot is or how much of a waste of time all this is, making your friend feel guilty.

Now consider the same situation, but instead of complaining, you directly talk about your hatred for horror movies, then ask if your friend would be willing to do any other movie marathon, perhaps a 007 movie marathon.

With the latter option, you avoid getting into a fight and protect your friendship from becoming toxic. With the former approach, your personality makes the relationship uncomfortable for everyone.

Let's consider another example where you have paired up with your competitive colleague for an upcoming project.

Here you have two options;

- Keep working with the same partner, risking the chance of acting out in anger during the presentation, risking your career, or,

- Talk with your manager about giving you another partner because you feel your work approach isn't compatible with your colleague's competitiveness.

By openly talking and expressing your feelings, you save yourself and other people from possible embarrassment. Avoid being passive-aggressive so that other people feel comfortable enough to want to build relations with you.

#: Be honest

Before you lie, always remember that relationships built on lies never last. Although lying may come easy, it has adverse long-term effects on relationships. We usually lie when we fear the consequences of the truth.

You keep the other person in denial by lying about your feelings or by hiding the truth. If you want people to give you genuine respect, you need to practice honesty with them.

Be honest about how you feel and never keep people in the dark, no matter the situation. By doing this, you can gain trust and earn respect.

#: Don't allow your jealousy to get the better of you

When you aren't happy or satisfied with your life, you start comparing your life to other peoples'. Self-comparison only leads to heartbreak and discontentment.

Here're somethings you can do to overcome jealousy:

- Practice gratitude by counting all your blessings. Anything that brings you happiness or you can have effortlessly is a blessing. Your life, job, family, and friends are all blessings you tend to ignore. Practice gratitude by noticing good things in your surroundings and appreciate them. When stress gets the best of you, making you question your life, close your eyes and think about your friends, family, and nature and be thankful for having such beautiful blessings in your life. You must also practice gratitude by appreciating and thanking others for their endless favors, showing them respect and value. Be content with yourself by practicing self-love.

- Tell yourself how amazing you are and just as unique as anyone else. Make positive affirmations like "I am the best" and "I believe in myself," and recall these five to ten times a day, boosting your self-confidence. You can also place notes with positive messages for yourself in different places, reminding you to practice self-love.

- Always help and support your loved ones at all times. Be happy for them and support them the same way they support you. Be sympathetic and become a reason for someone's happiness by sharing their grief and sorrow. Before passing judgment, always consider yourself in someone's situation and treat everyone how you'd want others to treat you.

- Moreover, train yourself to channelize your 'envy' positively by not reacting to it. When you sense it, acknowledge your feelings of jealousy for someone. Take deep breaths to calm down your intense emotion, and then think of how you can improve the resentment that builds inside you or use it to achieve something you want. For example, if you are jealous of your colleague getting one promotion after another because you want the same, identify your weak work areas and start improving them.

When you overcome jealousy, you attract positive people in your life and find it easier to overcome a toxic personality.

#: Put your ego aside

If you want to fight toxicity and stop being selfish, you need to put your ego aside. You protect your image by being defensive and attacking the self-esteem of other people.

You let your ego come in between your personal and professional life. Upon not getting enough appreciation and praise, you allow your ego to get the better of you, making you fight, argue, or physically harm other people.

However, you can follow these tips to manage your ego.

- Stop prioritizing yourself. Instead, give your loved ones the priority, love, and care they deserve.

- Critically observe your behavior and de-focus on other peoples' mannerisms; after all, you can only control what you do.

- Remember that it's okay to be wrong. Give yourself room for improvement and learn from your mistakes.

- Be more compassionate towards others by looking for ways to help people, greeting people nicely, smiling more at them, and saying words of encouragement and love to those in distress.

#: Be accountable

By taking accountability for your mistakes and bad behavior, you elevate your position and image. People start respecting you, sharing with you, and caring for you once they observe a positive change in you.

Here're some things you can do to become more accountable:

- Apologize when you are wrong. An apology tells other people that your ego no longer controls you, bringing them one step closer to you.

- Be honest about your wrongdoings. For example, if you have lied, cheated, or caused any other damage, you must accept it. By doing so, you reduce the chance of other people leaving you and increase the chances of building trust and receiving respect and honesty in return.

- If you promise to do something, do your best to do it. In case you cannot, take responsibility for that and make amends.

- Practice what you preach, and never ramble on about things you don't do. If you're not a fitness enthusiast, there is no need to portray yourself as one by overstating your love for being physically fit.

#: Develop empathy

A toxic mind can't think about others. However, if you want social acceptance, you need to be empathetic. Empathy means to feel the pain, sorrow, and grief of another person. Here are a few ways to develop empathy.

- Put yourself in other peoples' shoes. Imagine yourself helpless and needy, like the poor person begging you for money. When you put yourself in other peoples' situations, it becomes easier to relate to their pain.

- Be a good listener and support those in their grief. For example, if your friend feels upset because of his parent's sudden demise, spend time with him and hear him out; sometimes, presence can save someone's life.

- Always try to help others. By doing so, you engage yourself in a more positive activity rather than sitting alone and venting.

#: Do what's right, not what's easy

Life has many responsibilities that we're unwilling to take. If you're always running away from responsibilities, doing what's easy instead, you must learn to be accountable for your actions and mistake rather than accusing others, which seems to be an easy option. By doing so, you portray yourself as a responsible and trustworthy person.

For example, if your significant other complains and criticizes your behavior, the easy way is to start a fight or argument; the hard way is to accept your mistakes and make amends.

Choosing the right path can be tough, but it's better than choosing the wrong thing, going astray in the process.

#: *Exercise*

Nothing is as fun and easy as exercise. Physical activity increases endorphin hormones, pumping your blood, making you feel energetic and happy. Exercise reduces stress and toxicity because it diverts your attention from negative to positive aspects of life. You release stress with every move and breath you take. Ensure you schedule exercise in your daily routine to gain its long-term benefits.

Start with a few minutes of rigorous physical activity, then slowly increase the duration and frequency. Set a fixed time for it to build consistency, and if it helps, have a fitness partner; it'll help you remain motivated and committed.

Changing yourself is not hard; all it requires is time, consistency, and the willingness to improve yourself. Keep practicing the methods mentioned above and make them a part of your daily routine.

Since you now have a better hold on your emotions, let's discuss the icing on the cake: self-improvement:

Chapter 7: How to Identify and Overcome Your Weaknesses and Shortcomings

Identifying your weaknesses and shortcomings and overcoming them is one of the most important approaches towards self-betterment and your fight against defensive behavior.

You are not perfect, no one is, but you can always move a step closer towards betterment. You must be aware of your weaknesses and areas of improvement before you can effectively address them.

Recognizing your weakness shows the strength of your character and resolve. You can never improve if you believe your skillset is the best it can ever be. If people criticize you, they do it for a reason: they want you to succeed or because you lack a certain skill or an ability. Take criticism as a chance to correct yourself. Recall all the criticism and advice you get and start analyzing the changes that, when made, can foster self-improvement.

Let's dive into how you can identify your weaknesses and improve yourself.

How to Identify Your Weaknesses and Shortcomings

It takes a lot of courage to find faults in yourself. Be proud of the fact that you're working on identifying your shortcomings. Observe your performance at work and your ability to handle your emotions and see where you lag.

Ask yourself these questions to identify your weaknesses.

- "What am I good at?"
- "When and why do people criticize me?"
- "On which occasion did I require help from others?"
- "Which project, skill, and task drained my energy?"
- "In which projects have I invested more time and effort?"

While performing any task or activity, keep these questions in mind to find your weak areas.

#: List down your weak points

If you cannot give your 100% in any field, it means you need to improve in that area.

- List down everything you think needs improvement. Try recalling incidents that made you feel insecure or disappointed in your performance.

- Start organizing your weaknesses into categories. For instance, if you want to be more outgoing, positive, and confident, create a category entitled 'assertiveness skills.' Similarly, start making categories of all the skills you want to achieve or improve.

- Figure out the underlying causes of your weaknesses. For instance, if your productivity is slowing down, think of why you are experiencing this problem. If it is because you procrastinate a lot, think of why that happens. When you figure out your weaknesses' root causes, you understand the key areas you need to improve.

Go through these reasons severally to explore and comprehend your shortcomings better so you can tackle them accordingly.

#: Seek feedback

Sometimes you tend to ignore your weak points, not realizing the importance of improving them. You should always seek feedback about your performance and behavior because other people can view you with a critical view, pointing out your faults.

- Always seek feedback from those who show their loyalty and concern; they genuinely wish the best for you. Before presenting your work, show it to a friend who will help you improve by pointing your mistakes.

- Feedback helps you identify both your weakness and strengths. For example, make a questionnaire about yourself, including questions about your skills, abilities, and behavior, and have your acquaintances field it. The answers will help you analyze your areas of improvement.

#: *Identify underlying factors, problems, and issues*

You always blame yourself for not being capable enough to achieve your target, stressing yourself. You must realize you are not always at fault. Instead of blaming yourself, start searching for other factors that might act as barriers to your goals.

- **Environmental factor:** Perhaps you can't concentrate on your work because of the noise and distractions present in your surroundings? Try finding the perfect spot or spend some alone time where you can focus on yourself without any interruption.

- **Envious people.** Sometimes it's not you but your rivals who demoralize you, crushing your confidence. You must endeavor to ignore them and avoid their company so that you can focus fully on your goal.

- **Unhealthy Thoughts:** You may get distracted from your work or have bad habits caused by unhealthy thoughts. Identify those thoughts and replace them with positive ones. For instance, if you often think, 'I cannot grow beyond a certain point. There is no reason to put in more effort,' change it to, 'I can be better than ever. I can unlock my full potential if I continue working hard.' If you think you are perfect, remind yourself that nobody is perfect; we all have weaknesses that we need to improve by building new skills and becoming better in every way.

#: *Try new things*

Lacking experience is one of the reasons why many of us struggle to identify our weaknesses. Your growth starts when you push yourself to try things you have never experienced before. When you try something new, it helps you develop a new skill and observe which skill requires more effort. For instance, if you cannot complete a puzzle piece in the given time, it shows you need to improve your focus and concentration.

You can list down all things you haven't experienced and, upon experiencing them, categorize those skills as your strengths and weaknesses to have a better idea about what you need to improve.

Now that you have identified your weaknesses, it's time to start working on them.

How to Overcome Your Weakness and Shortcomings

Once you have identified your weaknesses, overcoming them is not too difficult. Start implementing these simple steps to improve yourself.

#: *Find a mentor*

Find a mentor who will guide and help you overcome your weaknesses and shortcomings. Your mentor can be your friend, spouse, therapist, or anyone you trust wholeheartedly. Your mentor must be someone who has seen you in various situations and is well aware of your ups and downs.

Look out for people who inspire you in various personal or professional capacities, people you wish to learn from, and then reach out to them. At first, some of these people may be hesitant about mentoring you. However, if you show your commitment to learning from them, they will eventually agree to guide you.

Allow your mentor to develop strategies you can use to overcome your flaws and turn them into strengths. Seek the person's advice when you encounter unforeseen obstacles that may cripple your self-improvement.

Ask your mentor to test you to your limits and make you submit to deadlines. You must trust your mentor and abide by his/her rules for efficient results.

When you work alongside a seasoned professional or someone you admire as a person, you open yourself to feedback and learning from someone else. Doing that lessens the severity of your defensive behavior automatically, allowing you to accept feedback and use it wisely for self-betterment.

If you cannot find a mentor from whom you can learn on a one-on-one basis, look for inspirational people online, find their podcasts, books, and lectures, and go through them until you learn what you need to make personal changes.

#: *Improve your skills*

Never set barriers on what you can or can't do; always push yourself to improve your skills and capabilities. The things you can't do with confidence or require assistance are your weaknesses. If you observe yourself, you can notice these areas and seek ways to improve.

Here're somethings you can do:

- Online classes. Life has become advanced, and you can now get everything online without the hassle of going outside. After identifying your weak areas, take lessons online, seek online consultation, or join Facebook groups for guidance and feedback. For example, if you love making crafts but don't have the know-how, you can always search for videos or DIY crafts in your free time, adding another skill to your accomplishment list.

- Your goal shouldn't be just learning a skill; it should be to master it. You tend to lose skills that you don't practice often. Thus, to retain a skill all your life, you need to master it.

- Once you have achieved your goal, set a new one. Don't ever quench your thirst for learning skills because you never know when you might require a specific skill. Don't waste your free time by lying around; instead, watch educational videos, listen to podcasts, attend classes online, and learn something new.

#: Watch how people act in your presence

How people act in or outside your presence says a lot about how your presence affects the environment. Observe whether, upon seeing you, people smile, become silent, show excitement, or ignore you.

If they show excitement and warmly welcome you, it means you have been successful t satisfying them emotionally and mentally. However, if people show resentment or act oddly but smile in your absence, it shows they are uncomfortable in your presence, which means you need to become more emotionally masterful. Be vigilant and observe how others treat you to find any areas of improvement.

#: Build confidence

Nothing is more important than self-reliance, confidence, and believing in yourself. You must believe you have what it takes to achieve your target. Lack of confidence distracts you, making you focus on your weakness instead of your strengths.

Here are a few ways to build self-confidence:

- Improve your body language. Don't slouch and maintain eye contact when you talk.

- Stand in front of the mirror and talk, focusing on your gestures and correcting your posture.

- Participate in healthy discussions, which gives you the confidence to share your ideas.

- Don't slouch when walking, standing, or sitting. Keep your back straight, shoulders open, and head held high. That is a high-power pose, and as Amy Cuddy's research shows, high-power poses increase testosterone levels. Testosterone is a hormone associated with confidence and enthusiasm; when its levels are high, you feel more self-assured and good about yourself.

- Improve your knowledge of your area of expertise. That way, when you speak, write or discuss it, you are aware of the different angles associated with it and can speak assertively.

#: *Learn time management*

At times it's not your skill or lack of confidence but your inability to manage time that leads to failure. How you manage work and schedule tasks by estimating their duration builds your image as a reliable and trustworthy employee. Being punctual and giving others your time shows how much you value them.

For example, you must manage your time well to ensure that you complete your everyday tasks and provide quality time to your significant other, showing how much you value him/her.

If you want to be effective, you must practice discipline, manage time, and be punctual. If time management is the area you need to improve, consider setting alarms, reminders, or downloading scheduling apps that remind you about your tasks.

#: *Research*

Life is all about learning new experiences that enhance your knowledge and well-being. You can always improve your skills by researching and studying how and why you should overcome those weak areas.

For example, if you lack communication skills, you can research the importance of this skill, then determine why and how you can develop it efficiently.

#: *Admit your mistakes*

You cannot improve if you keep denying your mistakes and weakness, believing you are perfect. To turn weaknesses into strengths, you must learn to accept them.

Thus, you should always recognize and determine your weakness.

- You need to admit you are not perfect and can make mistakes like every normal human being. Admit that and start putting efforts towards enhancing your skills.

- Please don't be too harsh with yourself; give yourself some space to identify your weakness and work on them. If you discover any weak points, don't label yourself as a weak or under-confident person. Instead, accept it gracefully and find ways to improve.

- When you receive criticism, remember that it's only because of your incompetence in that specific area. Take criticism as a challenge and prove others wrong by advancing that skill.

#: Utilize other peoples' skills

Mastering every skill is impossible. However, you can always hire someone to provide the skills you lack. There are a few exceptional cases where a person can perform every skill with great expertise. If you aren't one of them, you can always ask others for help.

For example, take an instance where you want to start an online business, but you lack experience in eCommerce management. In that case, instead of shifting your focus towards learning eCommerce management, hire an expert. By doing so, you won't give your weakness a chance to hinder your business growth. Doing this will compensate for your weakness and help you develop a new skill of building trusting relationships.

We live in an imperfect world where you have to accept that you are good at some things, average on others, and extremely lousy at some that are important. Remember, you can never excel at everything you do, and that's okay.

Just try focusing on building core skills like communication, building relationships, and others that help you survive. By overcoming your weaknesses, you stop being defensive and become a confident and self-sufficient individual.

Use these strategies to improve your weaknesses and note down all the positive changes you observe in yourself. Another factor that makes you who you are is your mindset. In the next chapter, we will discuss the growth mindset and how it can help you overcome defensive behavior:

Chapter 8: Growth Mindset: Why and How you Must Develop it

There is a reason why *"develop positive thoughts, not negative ones"* is so common a piece of advice. It is so because your thoughts turn into beliefs, developing a certain mindset. A mindset is a set of thoughts or beliefs based on how you perceive yourself and your life. Mindsets have two categorizations: fixed **mindset** and **growth mindset**.

You develop mindsets early in life, depending on your upbringing, experiences in life, and ability to act or handle a situation in a certain way. For instance, if you grw up learning that it's important to look smart and please people, you're likelier to have a fixed mindset. You become more concerned about how people perceive you, developing the fear of not living up to their expectations, which can cause you to live a rote life.

On the other hand, if you grew up learning the value of exploring, accepting challenges, and learning new experiences, you tend to develop a growth mindset. Instead of seeing your mistakes as setbacks, you learn from them and find new ways to succeed.

Moreover, your mindset also depends on self-suggestions. If you continuously limit your potential by thinking negative, limiting thoughts, you're likely to have a fixed mindset. However, if you encourage yourself, yours is likely to be a growth mindset.

Now let's individually discuss these two mindsets for better understanding.

What Is A Growth Mindset?

If you believe that you have what it takes to achieve your goals by putting in more effort to excel in life, you have a growth mindset. The never-ending thirst for knowledge and new skills is what we refer to as growth, and when you nurture a mindset that stimulates you to pursue growth, we call that having a 'growth mindset.'

When you have a growth mindset, you handle criticism positively and learn from your mistakes. You are always looking for opportunities to learn new skills, knowing that the more you learn, the more you will excel.

Importance of Growth Mindset

A growth mindset helps you create a positive lifestyle where you choose to learn from your experiences.

Positive lifestyle

A growth mindset helps you build a positive lifestyle by accepting challenges and criticism constructively. You readily accept your mistakes, believing you are not perfect and are willing to improve.

For instance, if your boss asks you to amend your report, you don't feel ashamed or angry; you take it as an opportunity to impress him with better work.

People easily get along with you and know you most for your positive nature and other endearing traits.

Builds confidence

Learning experiences improve your confidence. A growth mindset makes you confident enough to take new risks and face criticism boldly. As you learn, explore, and experience new things, you are vulnerable to criticism and hardships. You ignore these factors as you are confident enough in the knowledge that, with time and consistency, you're capable of triumphing over anything.

Master more skills

The drive to perfect one skill helps you learn a lot more skills in the process. For example, if you're working on your communication skills, in the process, you'll also learn new ways to develop self-confidence, overcome stage fear, and develop eye contact.

Now let's talk about the fixed mindset and understand how it limits your growth and makes you defensive.

How the Fixed Mindset Limits You

Having a fixed mindset means having a mental tendency to believe that you cannot change because you have certain core traits that you cannot improve. Fixed mindsets produce two types of individuals.

- **The overconfident:** You start to believe you are competent enough for every challenge, and even though you have outdated skills, you think you don't need to change or improve in any way. For instance, if you have two hours to prepare your speech, instead of jotting down the points and practicing communication skills, you spend the time relaxing, thinking you can easily deliver the speech without any practice. When you give a bad speech, instead of accepting your mistakes, you blame it on the audience's 'lack of understanding or the 'faulty PA system. That causes you to build defensive behavior that never allows you to accept your mistakes.

- **The under-confident:** You feel unworthy and fear facing challenges, considering yourself an unskilled person. You believe that you cannot learn anything new because you lack what it takes. For example, when you become a manager at work, you don't think you can move to a more senior position because you don't have the talent and skills to do so. Instead of polishing your current skills and developing new ones, you stay stagnant where you are, thanks to your fixed mindset. Since you believe that you lack the skills you need to prove yourself or move further in life, you feel unconfident. This lack of confidence sometimes makes you nurture a bitter and defensive attitude towards others.

Your mind focuses more when you receive praise and less when you're receiving criticism, which makes you defensive. Instead of focusing on what you learn, you focus more on how others perceive you.

Fixed Mindset in Action: The Tortoise and the Hare

Here, the tortoise and hare story is not about two animals; it's about the two mindsets. The hare represents a fixed mindset. Mr. hare was so certain of winning that he decided to sleep for a while. On the other hand, the tortoise, representing the growth mindset, decided to plod along, hoping he might win.

Upon waking up, the hare tried his best to catch up but couldn't win even with his innate ability to hop faster. The tortoise, who knew his weakness, aced it with confidence without thinking about failure.

That is how a fixed mindset limits you. A fixed mindset is also another factor that feeds your defensive attitude. Let's look at how.

Fixed mindset and defensive behavior

Fixed mindset and defensive behavior have many traits in common.

- **Overconfidence:** Overconfidence is often the cause of defensiveness. That's because considering yourself perfect makes you intolerant to people who criticize you.

- **Consider others as failures:** You consider people who don't have skills similar to yours as failures. You cleverly compete with the weaker ones to satisfy your ego, avoiding embarrassment.

- **Don't accept rejection:** Other people don't need to agree with everything you say or do. Your mind doesn't prepare you for rejection as you haven't faced one because of your fight and flight response.

If you want to get rid of a fixed mindset and develop a growth mindset, you must feed your mind positive thoughts. Your mind does what you instruct it to do; it operates based on the thoughts and beliefs you feed it.

Thus, you can use positive suggestions to overwrite a fixed mindset:

- Whenever you feel triggered or face any challenge, don't think, 'I can't do this.' Instead, try thinking, 'this is tough, but I can do it.' Always give your mind positive ideas and thoughts to work with because, as mentioned, your mind listens to what you say and think.

- Train your mind to accept challenges. Do something new and challenging every day so that your mind gets prepared to handle unplanned situations. For example, go for a solo-hike, which will teach your mind how to plan, focus, and develop survival skills.

- Experience things alone, because when you're always in someone's company, you start depending on others for help. Go outside, do something adventurous, taking one step towards growth.

How to Develop a Growth Mindset

To develop a growth mindset, make the following changes to your lifestyle:

#: *Focus on growth, not speed*

You must realize learning new skills and excelling takes time. Your focus must be on quality, not quantity. 'Jack of all trades, master of none,' don't be like Jack. Instead, be yourself and keep adding to your skills by mastering them first.

Please take things slow when learning new things. Focus on personal development by the trial and error method. Don't give up when you fail. Instead, appreciate yourself for the slightest success and keep practicing until you master new skills and yourself.

#: *Keep creating goals*

Your goals keep you motivated to learn more. Please continue creating goals for each task; that's the only way to achieve success. If you stop setting goals, you will feel demotivated or become overconfident, believing you are too good to learn more.

If you are working towards improving your work performance, build goals revolving around giving better presentations, completing projects on time, closing bigger deals, etc.

Similarly, set different goals related to your health, personal life, and relationships so that you continue flourishing in life and have something positive to work on in every aspect of life.

#: *Stop seeking external approval*

When you seek external approval from other people, you turn into a people pleaser, and in one way or another, you become dependent on outside validation to be happy. That limits your growth and plays a role in shaping your defensive behavior. It so happens that often, we become so frustrated when we don't receive the external approval we seek from others that we become bitter, which triggers our defensive behavior.

Whatever you do, it must be for your benefit. Seeking external approval stops your growth because it causes you to become co-dependent, behaving in ways that give you the approval you want at the detriment of things that improve your well-being.

Learn to be comfortable in your skin. Love and appreciate yourself for what you are by constantly telling yourself, 'I am proud of myself.' Appreciate your blessings and stop comparing yourself with other people.

Avoid excessive social media use because staying hooked to social media platforms leads to comparing yourself to what your social media friends choose to display to the world. It keeps you from being comfortable in your skin and wastes time you could otherwise use for self-improvement.

#: *Take challenges as an opportunity*

Without challenges, life gets boring and monotonous. Challenges add a little spice to your everyday routine, giving you a chance to use your abilities to their fullest or learn something new.

For example:

Imagine that your boss asks you to make an excel sheet, something you know nothing about or how to do. Instead of panicking, you can use the internet to look up how to complete the task, work on it by taking baby steps, and focus on completing as much of it as possible.

When you engage yourself in a task, you enjoy it, learn to turn the challenge in your favor, and end up learning a new skill that improves your self-belief.

#: *Replace failure with growth*

The secret behind every successful person is this: **they never stop moving forward despite multiple failures.**

You must realize and accept that failure gives you a golden opportunity to correct your mistakes before someone else does; it's a disguised friend meant to help you grow.

Here are some tips to improve your attitude towards failure and use your setbacks in life as chances for growth:

- Always have a positive attitude towards setbacks. Learn from your mistakes and take them as a chance to improve yourself.

- Hardships always teach you a lesson. If something doesn't go right, think of what it taught you and accept it happily.

- Understand that failure helps you turn your weakness into strengths.

#: Keep positive company

You have no doubt heard the famous saying, "your company determines your character.' Your company greatly influences your thinking ability.

Observe how different unhealthy influences in your social circle affect you, and slowly distance yourself from them. Simultaneously, spend more time with people who talk about growth, development, and encourage you to outdo your skills. Now keenly observe your thought process to identify your mindset.

Let's move to the last chapter and discuss some positive habits that can help you overcome defensiveness, grow, and move further towards a happy life:

Chapter 9: Positive Habits to Improve Defensive Behavior

Your habits directly affect your well-being and behavior. To further reduce toxic, selfish, and defensive behavior, you should commit to building positive habits and engaging in healthy, positive activities.

Here are some great habits to get you started:

#: *Sleep well and early*

A good night's sleep is essential for your well-being and overall health. Sleeping well improves your emotional well-being, physical health, and cognition and helps you function optimally.

On the other hand, insufficient sleep can make you grumpy, irritable, and easy to offend. It impairs your emotional balance and hinders your ability to make correct judgments.

When you sleep well and enough, you feel fresh and have a good sense of self-control. You must sleep for 6-8 hours per day for improved health.

To do that, set fixed sleeping and waking up times, and start going to bed about an hour before your bedtime. Engage in some soothing activity such as taking a warm bath or reading a good book to relax your body and initiate sleep easily.

Additionally, make sure your bed is comfortable to sleep on and switch off noisy gadgets and appliances before sleeping.

Mood improving foods

Your food choices significantly impact your overall health. A fun way to improve your mood is by eating foods rich in tryptophan, an amino acid that produces a mood-elevating hormone called serotonin.

Serotonin is a chemical that improves your mood and well-being. Dark chocolate, fish, dairy products, and nuts are a few examples of foods rich in tryptophan. Add such foods to your diet to boost your happiness. The calmer and more positive you feel, the less irritable and defensive you will behave.

#: Do things you enjoy

Go for a walk, call a friend, read a book, or do whatever makes you happy and diverts your attention away from negative energy to a positive activity. By doing so, you will find new ways to dispense negative energy, helping you become a happy go lucky person.

Every day, do something that brings a smile to your face. These little ways of enjoying life help soothe toxic and defensive tendencies, helping you feel better.

#: Be a good listener

Start hearing out other people instead of forcing them to listen to you. Being a good listener is a sign that you value and respect the other person. As you slowly build positive rapport with loved ones, they start to respect and love you. Naturally, when you receive love and attention from loved ones, you feel positive and control your defensive behavior.

Here are a few helpful tips you can use to improve your listening skills:

- Maintain eye contact with the person you are talking with, giving the person your complete attention.

- Be both physically and mentally present during a discussion. Sit with your shoulders upright instead of slouching.

- Do not fidget with your phone or watch while speaking to someone.

- Always give feedback at the end of the discussion.

Patiently listen to others so they may give you the same acceptance in exchange. Doing this fosters love and helps you form healthy relationships.

If you start working on these guidelines, you'll make your way to a happy life free from aggression, frustration, and toxicity.

Conclusion

This book is a complete guide on how to overcome defensive behavior. With the help of this book, you have learned not only about defensive behavior but also its other aspects.

Remember that patience and consistency are the keys to self-development. Thus, implement the guidelines we've discussed patiently and diligently. While practicing the methods, don't be too hard on yourself; give yourself time to adapt to the changes. Observe the changes you make or seek feedback from people who know you well.

Maintain an ongoing record of all the skills you know, the skills you want to learn, and your positive and negative habits. By keep track of yourself, you'll always know what you need to improve at any given time.

Good luck!

Printed in Great Britain
by Amazon

84809775R00050